Dichten =
Nr. 7

Sections I & II are taken from *Gesammelte Gedichte und Visuelle Texte*, Copyright © 1970 by Rowohlt Verlag GmbH, Reinbek bei Hamburg
Section III, from *Fenster,* Copyright © 1968 by Rowohlt Verlag GmbH, Reinbek bei Hamburg
Section IV, from *Reisefieber,* Copyright © 1989 Gerhard Rühm, published by permission of Rowohlt Verlag GmbH, Reinbek bei Hamburg
Section V, from *Geschlechterdings,* Copyright © 1990 Gerhard Rühm, published by permission of Rowohlt Verlag GmbH, Reinbek bei Hamburg
Section VI, from *Albertus Magnus Angelus,* Copyright © 1989 by Residenz Verlag, Salzburg und Wien

GERHARD RÜHM
i my feet
selected poems & constellations

translated from the German
by Rosmarie Waldrop

Burning Deck, Providence, 2004

DICHTEN = is a (not quite) annual of current German writing in English translation. Most issues are given to the work of a single author.
Editor: Rosmarie Waldrop.

Individual copies: $10
Subscription for 2 issues: $16
In England: £5.
Subscription for 2 issues: £8. Postage 25p/copy.

Distributors:
Small Press Distribution, 1341 Seventh St., Berkeley, CA 94710
1-800/869-7553; orders@spdbooks.org
Spectacular Diseases, c/o Paul Green, 83b London Rd., Peterborough, Cambs. PE2 9BS

for US subscriptions only:
Burning Deck, 71 Elmgrove Ave., Providence RI 02906

Some of the translations were first printed in *The Vienna Group: 6 Major Austrian Poets* (Barrytown, NY: Station Hill Press, 1985).

The publication of this work was supported, in part, by a grant from the Goethe-Institut.
Burning Deck is the literature program of Anyart: Contemporary Arts Center, a tax-exempt (501c3), non-profit corporation.

Cover image by Gerhard Rühm

© 1968, 1970 by Rowohlt Verlag GmbH, Reinbek bei Hamburg
© 1989, 1990 by Gerhard Rühm
© 1989 by Residenz Verlag, Salzburg und Wien
Translation © 2004 by Rosmarie Waldrop

ISSN 1077-4203
ISBN 1-886224-75-7

i my feet

CONTENTS

I. poems, constellations, ideograms 9 ——

II. text pictures 29 ——

III. windows 37 ——

IV. cabin fever: moscow 65 ——

V. genderally 73 ——

VI. albertus magnus 91 ——

I. POEMS
CONSTELLATIONS
IDEOGRAMS

from: *a heart in the left place: cool poetry* (1954) 11 —

poems (1954-69) ─────
the first half hour 12 —
i my feet 13 —
with him 14 —
europe 1954 15 —
irun... 17 —
a few things 18 —
affidavit 19 —
property equals theft 20 —
flower piece 21 —

constellations and ideograms (1954-64) ─────
night 22 —
in january 23 —
leaf 24 —
swallow 25 —
very 26 —
unite 27 —

documentary sonnet 28 —

a heart in the left place:
cool poetry

philologybrigida

•

a motorcycle
motors
like a modem

is that mormal?

•

I hop you believe me
or I'll have to hope up and down

•

stomps a boot through the night
my boot
forsooth
i have another boot
incredible
and on my head
grows hair

the first half hour
and
the second half hour
then
the whole following
and
the next following hour
and
another hour
and
yet another hour
and
yet more hours
and
always yet more hours
thus
it's
slowly
gotten to be
now
and
now
the first half hour
and
the second half hour
then
the whole following
and the next following

i
my feet
and you
your feet
walking
our feet
walking

i could also say other things
about other things

with him
who her
where i
through that
in at
for too
her most
and then
you half
who he
she it
there to
with him
who her
just half
so that

europe 1954

iceland
ireland
england
the netherlands border on germany and belgium
belgium borders on the netherlands, germany, luxembourg and france
luxembourg borders on belgium, germany and france
france borders on belgium, luxembourg, germany, switzerland, italy, monaco, andorra and spain
monaco borders on france
andorra borders on france and spain
spain borders on france, andorra and portugal
portugal borders on spain
italy borders on the vatican, san marino, yugoslavia, austria, switzerland and france
the vatican borders on italy
san marino borders on italy
switzerland borders on italy, france, germany, austria and liechtenstein
liechtenstein borders on switzerland and austria
austria borders on switzerland, liechtenstein, italy, yugoslavia, hungary, czecholsovakia and germany
germany borders on germany, austria, switzerland, france, belgium, the netherlands and denmark
denmark borders on germany
norway borders on sweden finnland and the soviet union
sweden borders on norway and finnland
finnland borders on sweden, norway and the soviet union
the soviet union borders on finnland, norway, corea, china, mongolia, afghanistan, iran, turkey, rumania, hungary, czechoslovakia and poland
poland borders on the soviet union, czechoslovakia and germany

germany borders on germany, poland and czechoslovakia
czechoslovakia borders on austria, germany, germany, poland, the soviet union and hungary
hungary borders on yugoslavia, austria, czechoslovakia, the soviet union and rumania
rumania borders on yugoslavia, hungary, the soviet union and bulgaria
bulgaria borders on rumania, yugoslavia, greece and turkey
yugoslavia borders on bulgaria, rumania, hungary, austria, italy, albania and greece
albania borders on yugoslavia and greece
greece borders on albania, yugoslavia, bulgaria and turkey
turkey borders on greece, bulgaria, the soviet union, iran, irak and syria

irunbreathlesslyacrosstheplainrollingyourheadinfrontofme

a few things

on the table
a grey tablecloth
on it an open pack of cigarettes
    shiny yellow torn blue
beside it a half-empty bottle of domestic kirsch
    (product of austria)
in front of that the typewriter with my fingers
to the left of it a ballpoint
a notebook (orange)
underneath a white sheet of paper with a poem
    title february
next to that (near the edge of the table) a shabby briefcase
    it's shut (but i know what's inside)
and when i'm not typing my right arm
    on the edge of the table
my face just about above it
it's 1 PM
the table will presently look different

eg there
will be our faces facing each other
our mouths opening and closing
our hands moving knife and fork
our eyes meeting now and then

so i've risked a few predictions for the next
    fifteen minutes
and end
with my eye
on the door

affidavit

I, Gerhard Rühm,
herewith declare under oath
that on crossing Kurfürstendamm
I inadvertently stepped in a puddle
spattering my practically new pants up to the knee.

Berlin, August 30 of the current year.

property equals theft

my hair
my head
my eyes
my ears
my nose
my mouth
my neck
my arms
my hands
my torso
my balls
my prick
my wife
my vagina
my thighs
my knees
my calves
my feet
my shoes
my world
my brain

flower piece
for günter brus

the tulip shits on the lawn
the violet farts in the gardener's hand
the forget-me-not vomits into the tissue paper
the pink sucks on its stem
the orchid masturbates between the missy's fingers and dribbles
on her arm up to the sleeve
the rose stinks of sweat and menstrual blood
the snowdrop snots on the fresh tablecloth
the lily pisses into the vase
the hyacinth gives a belch

night
and the daughter of night
and the daughter of the daughter of night
and the daughter of the daughter of the daughter of night

day
and the son of day
and the son of the son of day
and the son of the son of the son of day

the son
and
the daughter

and all their relatives all the relatives

look at the siblings

look at the son and the daughter
of the son and the daughter
of the son and the daughter

and it is day
and it is night

in january
as in autumn
it is thursday

in spring
it is wednesday
as early as eleven

while sunday
predominates
during winter and august

at noon
it is summer
and sometimes december

leafleafleafleafleafleafleafleafleafleafleafleafleaflea

swallow

s   wallow
sw   allow
s   wallow

swallow

s   wallow
sw   allow
s   wallow

swallow

very very very very very very very very very very very
very very very very very very very very very very very
very very very very very very very very very very very
very very very very very very very very very very very
very very very very very very very very very very very
very very very very very very very very very very very
very very very very very very very very very very very
very very very very very very very very very very very
very very very very very very very very very very very
very very very very very very very very very very very
very very very very very very very very very very very
very very very very very very very very very very very
very very very very very very very very very very very
very very very very very very very very very very very
very very very very very very very very very very very
very very very very very very very very very very very
very very very very very very very very very very very
very very very very very very very very very very very
very very very very very very very very very very very
very very very very very very very very very very very
very very very very very very very very very very very
very very very very very very very very very very very
very very very very very very very very very very very
very very very very very very very very very very very
very very very very very very very very very very very
very very very very very very very very very very very
very very very very very very very very very very very
very very very very very very very very very very very
small

```
        unite                    unite
         unite                   unite
          unite                  unite
           unite                 unite
            unite                unite
             unite               unite
              unite              unite
               unite             unite
                unite            unite
                 unite           unite
                  unite          unite
                   unite         unite
                    unite        unite
                     unite       unite
                      unite      unite
                       unite   unite
                        unite unite
                         uniteunite
                          unitunite
                           unite
```

> **documentary sonnet**
> **monday 21/7/1969**
> **the first men on the moon**

on súnday thé twentwénthiéth julý
nuníneteenhúndredsíxtyníne at át
eightéighteen mínutútes past níne at át
PM the twó américán julý

astástronáutauts néil neil árm julý
neil ármstrong ánd edédwin áldrin át
on bóard board óf the rócket 'éagle' át
landánded ón the plánet móon julý

they bóth both hád to páss five fíve more hóurs
in thé secúritýty óf their lánd
ing cápsulúle befóre they ás the hóurs

fifírst inhábitántants óf the lánd
the plánet éarth could sét their féet on hóurs
on ón a stránge celéstial bódy lánd.

II. TEXT PICTURES

bleiben

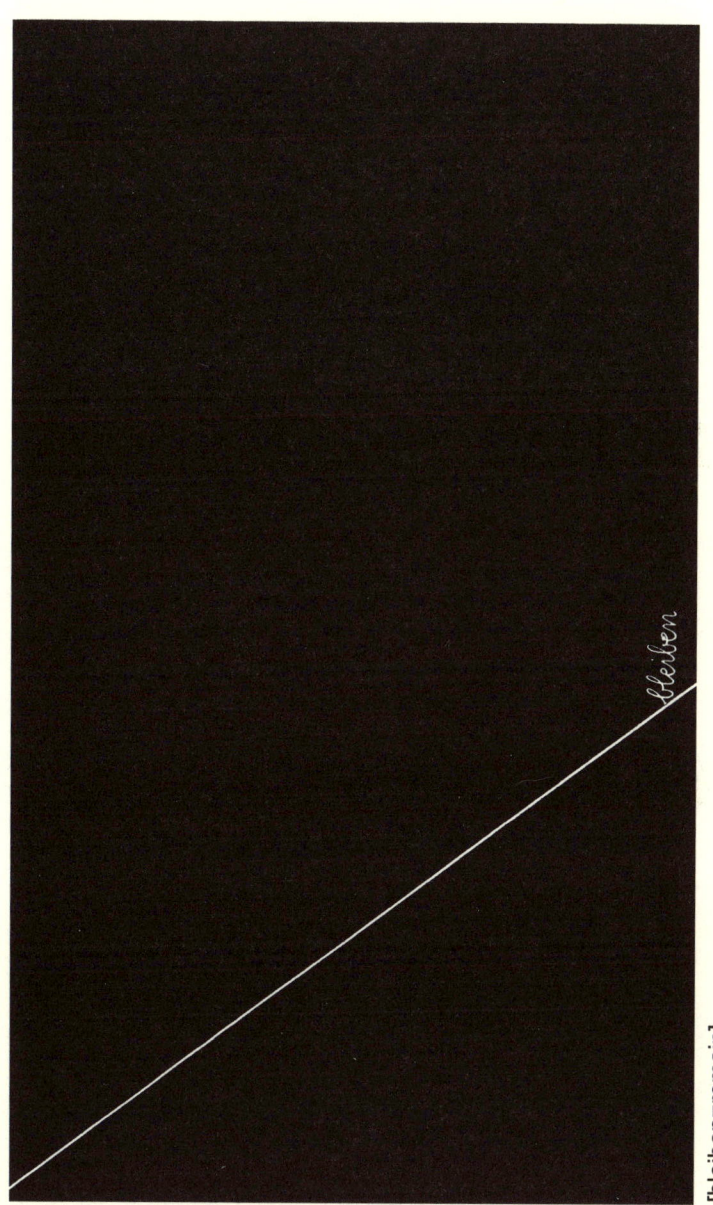

[bleiben=remain]

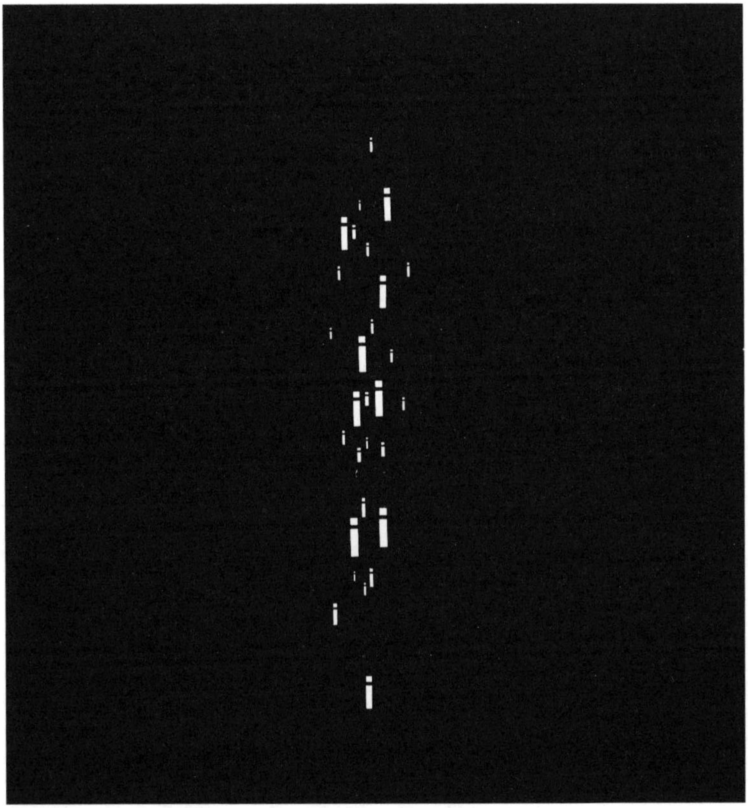

!
b i a
i b 0 d
b 0 i i O d
o i a
b b o O a o g d
p d
b p o i o d i a
p 0 i g g
b p i 0 g
p o

——— III. WINDOWS

splendor and misery of francesca da rimini 39 —

short excerpt from the life of franz maier 43 —

f. a. in vienna 50 —

the folded clock 58 —

*splendor and misery
of francesca da rimini*

she withdraws from the guests and, right after, a muted fall is heard outside. it is not by accident that the woman's brain is haunted by thoughts the bayreuth master has developed. we are led to francesca's room which is penetrated by cool night air. paolo opens a trap door. then the husband, determined to go to extremes, rushes off with his one-eyed brother. on the portrait of the statue we see an unusually strong broad-shouldered man with short neck. while we gild the tassels, he tries to assume that air of enthusiasm that theseus, duke of athens, has called sweet madness. droysen makes do with swiss dialect, wilbrandt with that of upper bavaria. it is true that donato fell into the rhine, but did not die and will soon return as a man of substance. francesca is confused and excited because the dream threatening her with catastrophe recurs again and again. the reporters are turned back at her door, unconsoled, and the other rumors about her are either mere guesswork or downright invention. in the encyclopaedia she was born in 1827, in reality in 1823. she does not for a moment think that she could be overcome by indisposition or attacked by a hooligan. as a german, one is a bit annoyed how arbitrarily any truth and possibility is stood on its head just for the sake of effect. also, the dancer's name is not essler but elssler no matter how difficult these four consonants might find it to roll off a parisian tongue. the old warrior puts on the bearskin hat of the napoleonic gard and shoulders the rifle of that period. now follows a scene that easily matches even the most extravagant inventions of the romantic school. his mask has, by the way, been faultlessly reproduced in rubber. he demands that his cradle be brought in. what will he do? if he swings from the tree down to the ground and tells the fairy tale of the moon he will control the situation with sovereign humor. a green sardine comes into view, opening up from the middle. paolo steps forward, describes the pleasures of hunting and asks that this crude little play not be taken for more than the offspring of carefree whimsey. shortly after, we see the infant carried off with horrible wounds on its abdomen. a lord and his confidant, both speaking in iambic pentameter, think up a joke. the love of nature inspired this fragrant and emotional work. paolo however learns for the first time what it means to be sick, poor and helpless. his egotism melts when a girl of the people, almost a child, in religious ecstasy wants to do for him what only the purest love can achieve. to sacrifice herself unto death, to give her heart's blood is after all the highest happiness of every woman. the master counsels the girl to think it over once more before she sacrifices herself. he describes vividly the terrible things in store for her, how he, in spite of her virginal modesty, would undress her, tie her arms and legs, and tear her heart from her breast. but the girl mocks the doctor's doubts and replies: "i be a woman an i ha the strengthe." rich to excess, cloth, lace and silks are heaped before the eye of the beholder. sudden lightning flashes through a world agitated to the core. while she seems pervaded by an emotion promising utter happiness, a broken fan elicits the same tears from her as the thought of separation and death. but even this torture and execution involves a risk whose brave assumption merits recognition because it means the conquest of an entirely new field of poetry. the audience however is slow to warm up. it is unfair to the artist who knows to modulate his organ in many ways, to sound head or chest tones as required, to make it swell with emotion or fade to a mere breath in throw-away passages. with a wonderfull aria of lament the girl enters the other world. paolo suddenly finds himself alone in a darkened room. sings, crosses his heart, and asks in a childlike manner: "but this is not how it's supposed to be — or? or?" and dies in his turn of and with this question. the brother, one-eyed as he is, wants to climb the bell tower and announce to all the world what miracle has happened. all hear: "alleluja alleluja" from the church and, deeply moved, fall on their knees. enter francesca, slowly, sick and aged, in a long white robe. with pious jubilation she tried to lift the house off its walls. but in vain. there is something mysterious and inexplicable in the air which depresses her. while we try to strike one another with the bells her husband keeps pointing to the mud to remind us of the poverty and meanness of life, and on it a tender fragrant flower opening its petals to the light. (i am of course aware that this kind of soul analysis is dangerous and triggers all sorts of misunderstandings and indelicate mis-interpretations in certain readers who look for crude similarities between the story and reality.) finally we approach the dreadful end in prison where francesca has almost lost her capacity for speech. she is for the first time visited by her mother who robs her for good measure, while the prison director cracks the coarsest jokes about the inmates to the visiting lord and his confidant. standards are very low, by the way, striking dress and elegant onlookers most rare. at first we are fascinated by the idyll in the woods near paris (who could forget the old swashbuckler) where the murder took place. instead of some intolerable wooden podium we see an accurate replica of the lawn and trees as well as the flowery hill with its shady spots. to the left and right a group of extras busy eating their sandwiches. it seems the threatening catastrophe can no longer be averted. will francesca and her husband also die? we hope not, enough blood has been shed. (such occasions often lead to a row backstage in which every single person wants to be the winner.) meanwhile the brother has turned into a hooligan who scratches dimes together for beer, wolfs down whole baskets of bread and draws careless caricatures. he has made himself a laughingstock with his crush on the innkeeper's daughter who laughs at him and grants her favors to one of the customers. it seems unavoidable: he'll come to a bad end. now we can return to francesca and her husband. the latter gets more and more obnoxious and provoking. in a sudden fit of passion he pulls a gun from his pocket and takes aim, all the while wearing Beethoven's well-known death mask. suddenly an abrupt fall down the open trap door ends his young life. well then. francesca faces the dreadful echo of a fall into nothingness. how will she react? for the moment she is silent, a veritable pillar of salt. almost a mythic figure. donato appears in the shape of a water sprite. son of god that he is, he has bared his heart in his powerful art. his immense talent for transsubstantiation is evident. francesca does not recognize him. she is only aghast. so she asks her mother question after question, speaks of a master in salerno who heals with blood, and with a shudder picks up the long kitchen knife her mother has dropped. from here on, the mother on donato's arm, who seems to be the victim of miscalculation, will more and more fade into the background until she vanishes from sight. francesca can think of nothing but the knife. her fate is sealed. the lord and his confidant leave the autumnal garden on iambic pentameters, not without having put a wilted leaf in their lapels. wistfully we remember the great fanny elssler. her figure of light will, an auspicious star, lead us on our way through life...

short excerpt
from the life of franz maier

where the water table surfaces in the desert oases form.
i see where africa is located.
where storms come from is what meteorologists find out.
where his money comes from nobody knows.
where the goths migrated we learned in school.
we learned where the germanic tribes migrated.

it is so cold, as if it were winter.

i walk till i am tired.

mother told him: stop it; nevertheless he did it.
grandmother called after him not to lose the money; nevertheless he lost it.
cold, colder, coldest.
warm, warmer, warmest.
fresh, fresher, freshest.
salty, saltier, saltiest.
gloomy gloomier, gloomiest.
because of the shortness of life one should use every single moment.

a brave knight, clad from head to toe in iron, is riding, with open visor, through a dark rocky gulch.
presenting my profound respects i remain your humble and devoted servant franz maier.
as yesterday.

he entered the room without knocking at the door.
he saluted without taking off his hat.
he sat down without waiting to be asked.
he took of the food without saying thank you.

he talked without paying attention to what others said.
he left without saying goodbye.

the air is still and quiet.
it is snowing heavily.
you scream.
yesterday i was hoarse.

the lion is strong.
the birds are singing.
the storm is raging.
the air is so still and quiet, not a leaf stirring.

the boy turned back from fear of storms.

the boy turned back because he had great fear of storms.

the boy was afraid of storms, therefore he turned back.

the boy turned back because he was afraid of storms.

bark.
burke.
cork.
clerk.
kirk.
irk.
purple.
to grow into the infinite.
to drive into the greenery.
to look into the blue.
we went to melk to visit the monastery.
we go for a walk.
symmetry halves the connecting line between two points and is perpendicular to it.
dark and rough bodies absorb heat rays better than bright and smooth ones. (clothing.)

he feels the cold.
how dew forms.
from which direction the wind blows the weathervane shows.
i reply, i'm so tired i could drop.
dance, dander.
ditch, diptich.
smile, simile.
house, housewife.
wifeless.
lesson.
onward.
wardance.
dance hall.
hall light.
lighthouse.
it was a winter day.

three, five, eight, ten, seventeen, thirty-five, eighty.
the third, the fifth, the eighth, the tenth, the seventeenth, the thirty-fifth, the eightiest.
threefold, fivefold, eightfold, tenfold, seventeenfold, thirty-fivefold, eightyfold.
threesome, fivesome, eightsome, tensome, seventeensome, thirty-fivesome, eightysome.
a third, a fifth, an eighth, a tenth, a seventeenth, a thirtyfifth, an eightieth.
three-square, five-square, eight-square, ten-square, seventeen-square, thirty-five-square, eighty-square.
the trees are budding.
i stumbled and broke my leg.
franz tried to walk and fell down.
the heron froze and adapted to the environment.
grandmother.
decorated.
i went by car.

the voices were too far off.

. . heated were. . wares. .
. . heated were. . wares. .
. . heated were. . wares. .
whirling wind.
falling leaves.
pouring rain.

quickly he put his blotter over the spot.
with a bow he handed his bluebook to the teacher.
but the teacher said: stop fooling around, i saw you messed up your bluebook.
it snows so hard that you can barely see three steps in front of you.
in summer the telegraph wires hang slack. why?

here, there.
out, in.
up, down.
outside, inside.
to, fro.
right left.
in front, in back.
lead, follow.
forward, backward.
upward, downward.
uphill, downhill.
day in, day out.
they first walked around the park and then asquare the swan lake.
to be up in arms.
to throw down the gauntlet.
to look daggers.
to keep your powder dry.
to rattle your saber.
to get up on your high horse.
to break a lance for.
to go great guns.
to ask pointblank.

to entrench yourself.
to hang fire.
to stick to your guns.
to bite the bullet.
to be disarmed.
to be avantgarde.

wash your hands several times a day.
the sleeve hung down over the arm.
a singer sang an aria.
it is more than five hundred years ago that, in constance, johann huss was burned as a heretic.
we look in the direction the train is supposed to come from.

it started to rain, but luckily we had brought an umbrella.
he mostly drinks löwenbräu and at the end of dinner loves some emmenthal.
he went to bed without being sleepy.

to tell.
to hear.
to rustle.
to be silent.
to go.
to turn.
to remark.
to walk.
to say.
to pull.
to wander.
to crawl.
to seek.
to take.
to follow.
to hold.
to stay.
to forget.

to ask.
to look.
to force.
to lose.
to watch.
to note.
sundays i always sleep till nine o'clock.

most of the graves were beautifully decorated.
soon we came to my grandparents' grave.
we put down our bouquet, lit the candles and prayed.
my mother cleaned the grave lantern, meanwhile i arranged the flowers.
then we went back home.
all the streets of vienna put end to end would approach the distance from vienna to cairo.

a new year has begun, and everybody has the best intentions.
i too will pluck up courage and eagerly begin the new year.

i fell and injured myself, but the wound no longer hurts.
i must however stay in bed a while longer.

the danube comes from the black forest and flows into the black sea.
in the fall, our migrating birds migrate to the warm south.

before i go to bed i wash.
after i have washed i go to bed.
squeak, squeaked, squeaky
wheel gets the oil.
something whiter.
something stupider.
something mysteriouser.
by fits and starts.
time passes unnoticed.
i couldn't believe it was already eight o'clock.

the train arrives in the arrival hall of the station.
the travelers descend from the cars.
the arrivals see their acquaintances on the platform.
they cordially say hello.
the travelers hand in their tickets.
everybody leaves the station.
people disperse in all directions.
quiet returns to the square in front of the station.

                                        (july 1959)

f. a. in vienna

*for friedrich achleitner my friend
(23 may 1959)*

we walk very quickly next to one another we walk quickly away
from one another we walk toward one another we walk very
slowly past one another we walk slowly one behind the other
we walk with one another we walk very quickly we walk quickly
we walk very slowly we walk slowly we walk we walk we walk
very quickly next to one another so long we walk quickly away
from one another so long fritz we walk toward one another fritz
and i are friends we walk very slowly past one another fritz and
i are good friends we walk slowly one behind the other fritz and
i are very good friends we walk with one another so long we
walk very quickly we walk quickly we walk very slowly we walk
slowly we walk we walk WANDER we walk very quickly next to one
another WADDLE we quickly walk away from one another WAIT
we walk toward one another WASH we walk very slowly WADE
past one another we walk slowly one behind the other WAKE
we walk with one another WAVE we walk very quickly we walk
quickly WILT we walk very slowly we walk slowly we walk we walk
we walk very quickly next to one another we walk quickly away
from one another we walk toward one another we walk very
slowly past one another we walk slowly one behind the other
we walk with one another we walk very quickly WAKE we walk
quickly WARM we walk very slowly WHITE we walk slowly we
walk WARY we walk we walk very quickly next to one another
we walk quickly away from one another we walk toward one
another we walk very slowly past one another we walk slowly
one behind the other we walk with one another we walk very
quickly next to one another we walk quickly away from one
another we walk toward one another we walk very slowly past
one another we walk slowly one behind the other we walk with
one another we walk very quickly WAKE we walk quickly
WARM we walk very slowly WHITE we walk slowly we walk

WHEN

WARY we walk WOODS we walk very quickly next to one another WALL we walk quickly away from one another we walk toward one another WATER we walk very slowly past one another WILDERNESS we walk slowly one behind the other we walk with one another WIND we walk very quickly WINTER we walk quickly WHIPPOORWILLS we walk very slowly WEATHER we walk slowly we walk we walk WANDER we walk WAKE very quickly next to one another WOODS we WADDLE walk quickly away from one another WARM we walk toward one another WALL we walk very slowly past one another WAIT we walk slowly one behind the other we walk with one another WHITE we walk very quickly we walk quickly WATER we walk very slowly WASH we walk slowly WARY we walk WAX we walk WADE we walk WAKE very quickly WIND next to one another we walk WAKE quickly away from one another we walk toward one WARM another WINTER we walk WAVE very slowly past one another WHITE we walk slowly one behind the other we walk with one another WHIPPOORWILLS we walk very quickly WILT we walk quickly we WARY walk very slowly we walk slowly WEATHER we walk we walk how long can we walk without trouble five minutes fifteen minutes half an hour without limit we stand next to one another we stand one behind the other we stand opposite one another we sit down we sit opposite one another we sit next to one another we sit one behind the other we get up so long we walk very quickly next to one another so long we WANDER walk quickly WAKE away from one anWOODSother we WADDwalkLE toward WARM one anWALLother WAIT so long we walk very slowly past one another WHITE we walk WATslowlyER one behind the other WASH WARY so long we walk with one another so long we walk very quickly we walk quickly WILDERNESS so long

WHY

WHAT

W A L K

WHO   WHILE

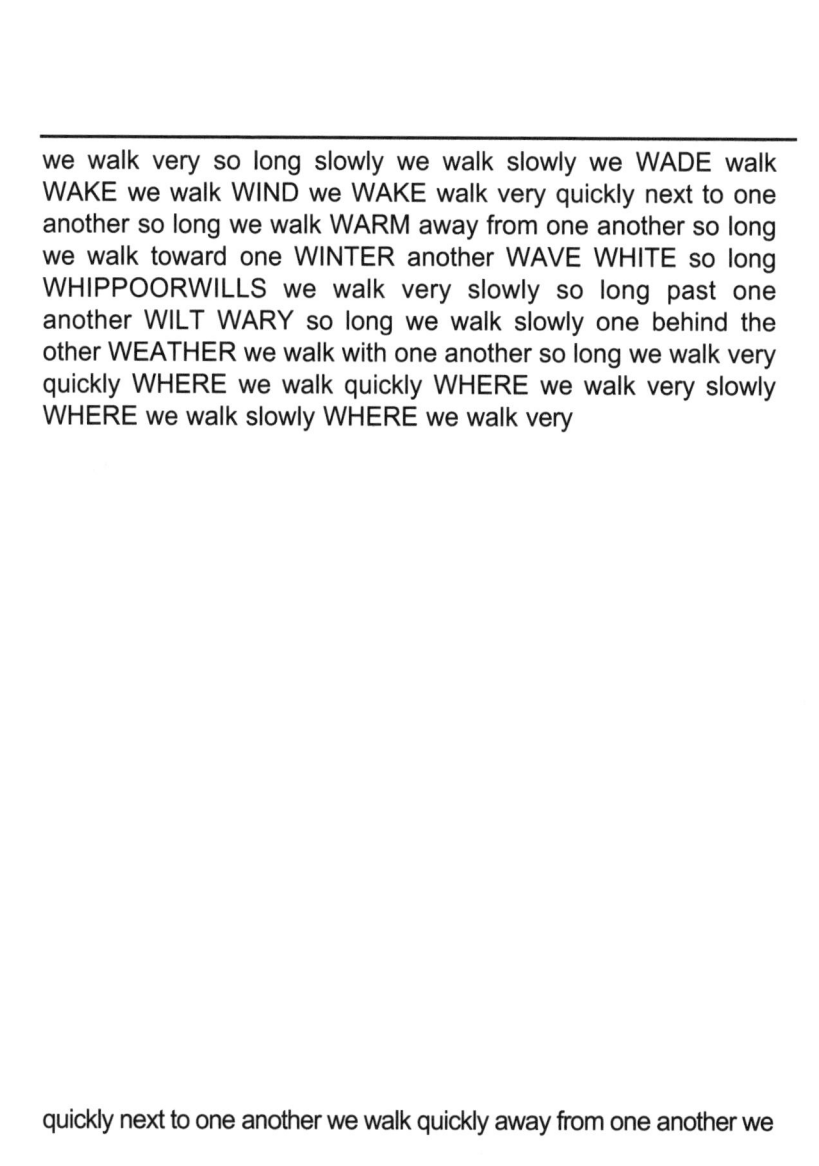

we walk very so long slowly we walk slowly we WADE walk WAKE we walk WIND we WAKE walk very quickly next to one another so long we walk WARM away from one another so long we walk toward one WINTER another WAVE WHITE so long WHIPPOORWILLS we walk very slowly so long past one another WILT WARY so long we walk slowly one behind the other WEATHER we walk with one another so long we walk very quickly WHERE we walk quickly WHERE we walk very slowly WHERE we walk slowly WHERE we walk very

quickly next to one another we walk quickly away from one another we

the folded clock
for m.

twelve possibilities
something has changed

eleven possibilities
different blue

something has changed
ten possibilities

for the first time
different blue

something has changed
nine possibilities

the unexpected
for the second time

different blue
something has changed

eight possibilities
the universe is expanding

the expected and the unexpected
for the third time

different blue
something has changed

seven possibilities
grey on grey

the universe is expanding
the expected and and the unexpected

for the fourth time
different blue

something has changed
six possibilities

yes or no
grey on grey

the universe is expanding
the expected and and and the unexpected

for the fifth time
different blue

something has changed
five possibilities

does one of us turn on the light when it gets dark
yes or no

grey on grey
the universe is expanding

the expected and and and and the unexpected
for the sixth time

different blue
something has changed

four possibilities
a reunion

does one of us turn on the light when it gets dark
yes or no

grey on grey
the universe is expanding

the expected and and and and and the unexpected
for the seventh time

different blue
something has changed

three possibilities
the found the invented

a reunion
does one of us turn on the light when it gets dark

yes or no
grey on grey

the universe is expanding
the expected and and and and and the unexpected

for the eighth time
different blue

something has changed
two possibilities

to go on together
the found the invented

a reunion
does one of us turn on the light when it gets dark

yes or no
grey on grey

the universe is expanding
the expected and and and and and and the unexpected

for the ninth time
different blue

something has changed
one possibility

something is being changed
different blue

for the tenth time
the expected and and and and and and and the unexpected

the universe is expanding
grey on grey

yes
one of us turns the light on when it gets dark

the reunion
the found the invented

to go on together
different blue

for the eleventh time
the expected and and and and and and and and the unexpected

the universe is expanding
grey on grey

yes
one of us turns the light on when it gets dark

the reunion
the found the invented

to go on together
for the twelfth time

the expected and and and and and and and and and the unexpected
the universe is expanding

grey on grey
yes or no

one of us turns the light on when it gets dark
the reunion

the found the invented
to go on together

the expected and and and and and and and and and and and
    the unexpected
the universe is expanding

grey on grey
yes or no

one of us turns the light on when it gets dark
the reunion

the found the invented
to go on together

the universe is expanding
grey on grey

yes
one of us turns the light on when it gets dark

the reunion
the found the invented

to go on together
grey on grey

yes
one of us turns the light on when it gets dark

the reunion
the found the invented

to go on together
yes

one of us turns the light on when it gets dark
the reunion

the found the invented
to go on together

one of us turns the light on when it gets dark
the reunion

the found the invented
to go on together

the reunion
the found the invented

to go on together
the found the invented

to go on together
to go on together

(1966)

IV. CABIN FEVER: MOSCOW

action	speaker	loudspeaker	projection
			[writing:] AHEM
a lamp-shade appears, followed by an abbot.			
		(speaker:) aberration, abatement: abessinian subscriber added.	
abbot:	aborigine abraham, robber of an apricot, in case of election fatigue, by all means abscond !		
		abstract nonsense.	
	abscess, so that the advance guard will in advance of the ramp of adventurers, the frequency of accidents in august at the air base likely to be australian austrian or autobiographical, by bus by offset by author with fountainpen, yes, an agate agent, lamb of god in agony on a landowner's aggressive husbandry, hell and adam as tone arm via administrative channels reach		
			[writing:] ADDRESS
	the adriatic by dinner time. in a — transparent—speculation on bills of exchange he plays the inno-cent who can't count to three and gambles alphabetically, this		

action	speaker	loudspeaker	projection
	asia minorian from the asov sea, this nitrogen compound, this stork! oh my, oh my! quinces! well then, my dear academics, this is the a-pronunciation of the unstressed o in acacia, the academy for communist education as watercolor, made to feel at home by the addition of a of a...[searches for the word]	[music:] accordeon	
	certified accumulator! punctually with shoulder strap, in this act as an actor, he supports the acting of the actress; a shark in accoustics, a midwife, he accepts any action. algebraic alabaster in red-checked peasant shirt. blushing, algerian, dying for a drink—well symbolically an avenue of whitewash at the speed of a diamond and an aloe approaching the altar of a three kopek coin. a skinflint, an alchemist of greed, a purple petrel in my family bible alcove as well as in the alpine almanach, with an alto voice as altimeter in light alloy and a coarse riding-habit from the amazon. daisy of sports fans, reservoir of ambition. embrasure in the surgeries of amoebas and americans.	[chorus:] amen.	
	after ammonia amnesty he amortizes the amperemeter. specialization: amputation. gear for love affairs: an amphibious		

action	speaker	loudspeaker	projection
	truck through the ranks, however analog the pineapple analysis of anarchy.		[slide:] anatomic drawing
	excommunication!	[speaker:] aircraft hangar. england. angora goat. the andes. anecdote. anemia. anemone. anesthesia.	
			[writing:] ANIMAL PAINTER
	anisette from ankara. appropriate the questionnaire by force and void it!	[speaker:] anode. anomaly.	
	an anonymous ensemble in conflict with antarctica. an unhealthy antenna toward antiquity. antiquarian antelopes from the antilles. antiphaty against anthologies of late apples and anthrax.		
			[writing:] PAUSE
	contractors and cannibals in flight of stairs from a upas tree with anchovy.		
enter annie,			

action	speaker		loudspeaker	projection
apathetic, holding pansies. she is wearing an open wing collar round her neck, nothing else.				
	annie:	i appeal to the apple		
			[sound:] applause	
		far from the earth, against the incredible indifference toward political things: apollo, defend the apoplexy of the apostles!		
	abbot:	apotheosis of the administrative apparatus, appendicitis not inhibiting the appetite. paste-up and make-ready in april.		
				[writing:] APOTHE-CARY
		arabian sea, arrak and arbitrary police actions deal with negroes in two-wheelers — no arbitration, just watermelons, wild sheep, noble steeds and argentina. argonaut slang offers proof against the tenants' arrest. ribwort, ariadne's thread, arian or arithmetical aria of bow and arrow. arctic harlequin in an armenian soldier's uniform. army in coats of durum wheat with aroma of arum and arsenic. relcalcitrant artesian wells of the		

action	speaker	loudspeaker	projection
	workers' syndicate. arteriosclerosis from articulating "artillery" and "artichoke." arthritis in the ammunition dump of the harp of the archangel of archeological archivists. the archbishop of the archipel writes "architecture" in giant letters. aqueduct of the rear guard, outstanding pilot of asbestos and antiseptic bandages, ascaris, the eelworm of school-slates, applicant to the general assembly of the united nations. garbage men advise and assimilate assyrians in an assortment of autonomous socialist soviet republics in association with asters. astrologers and astronomers on the asphalt. hey? what? how's that? the leaders attack the house of fashion with atmospheric pressure. an atlas of athletes in atomic range. atrophied organs of automatic dialing. advanced degree of hunting calls: hollo! hollo! huzza! huzza! damn! in the auditorium of "as the question so the answer" an auction of afghan villages, confidence deals, athens on the playbill, an axiom for africans. alas, groans the achilles heel. awful, not adequate at all, the ventilation in this airport!		

V. GENDERALLY

inventions 75 —

tuesday 77 —

digression concerning contemporary apartments 80 —

description of nature 81 —

the shortest route from constanz to constantinople 82 —

group dynamics 83 —

nature morte 85 —

litany for good friday 86 —

lovesong for lily 87 —

susanna's rhyming compulsion 88 —

inventions

apollo is the soap of automats
night a damp ruler measures the distance between flax
    and renunciation
a rope of blood and an anchor of bouncing balls are cast
    elastic corals crowd into the bar
gas keys and clarinets form the dregs of hope
corpses umbrellas and bagels drop from unbuttoned blouses
leap years are the romance of barbarism

•

the minuet in genesis
the raven of excrement
inez the loud and soft
candles of liver
a bow to the oviductor's falsetto
eplileptic nymphs
mermaids of razor blades
death as a preposition
photographed in a smiling star
between two and three quarters salt
late by one wart

•

father is an avenue of ultramarine
plains of bolts and nuts and halibuts of scars
inside find four hectoliters and the renaissance
thursday of aspic
the pocket watch tocks from cocks that fall out of socks
wind is an axe made of apples
egg yolk is an etude for the left gland

masked rocks with cancellation stamps escape into an operetta
(nobody will look for them here)
one tumor two jaguars one december and one septet climb out
   of a proverb reciting at great volume
a gentleman in a top hat hastily travels to tunisia
out of the songbook silent spaghetti

a carrier pigeon a comma a rotten tooth a greek myth no hope
   and many ask with some justification
w h y

(1954)

tuesday

my parents made me a present of tuesday
made a virtue of tuesday
in broad tuesday
between tuesday and the deep blue sea
tuesday is contagious
we yawn and in comes tuesday
in the tuesdays of old
carry the tuesday
fall on evil tuesdays
tuesday it up
man proposes tuesday disposes
bend over tuesdayward
live for tuesday
die for tuesday
every dog has his tuesday
a good tuesday's work
if you sow tuesdays you'll harvest tuesdays
a man cannot be in two tuesdays at once
tuesday to whom tuesday is due
be blind on tuesday
be deaf on tuesday
be completely paralyzed on tuesday
try to forget tuesday on tuesdays
tuesday tuesday everywhere
turn into a little tuesday yourself
imagine there's nothing outside tuesday
escape with your naked tuesday
from one tuesday to another
every tuesday
every duesday
the year has three hundred sixty-five tuesdays
no day without tuesday

he didn't see the week for the tuesdays
one tuesday much like another
spend your evening in the company of tuesdays
clink glasses with tuesday
get nowhere with tuesday
an embarrassment of tuesdays
let's call it a tuesday
screaming bloody tuesday
don't tuesdaydream
tuesday as second nature
it's tuesday
what will the next tuesdays have in store
get the paper and read tuesday
tuesday tuesday tuesday
divide tuesday into hours minutes and seconds
set your watch for tuesday
because it's tuesday
because it's tuesday
waste your life on tuesdays
stake everything on tuesday
move heaven and tuesday
see tuesday slip through your fingers
sleep
wake while tuesdays spread like rabbits
tuesday covers the land
he wouldn't give me the time of tuesday
postcards and pictures of tuesday
tuesday is my uncle franz
it's tuesday's fault
the tuesday hanging over your head
the tuesday at her breast
put a brave tuesday on it
tuesdays make a man of you
at the crack of tuesday
refuse something because it goes against all tuesday
the tuesdaily telegraph
my tuesdaily earnings

bravo tuesday
I thank you from the bottom of my tuesday
this is beyond the call of tuesday
never enough of a good tuesday
one good tuesday deserves another
dear tuesday
honored tuesday
esteemed tuesday
sufficient unto tuesday are the worries thereof
good tuesday
how do you tuesday
till tuesday then
almost forgot it's still tuesday

(1957/59)

digression concerning contemporary apartments

mamma sits in the closet and cries
baby opens the door
daddy shuts it
the carpet is of washable china
in the vase a mortgage
a fly crawls up the window pane
nylon mist
yes out there
what does baby say to daddy
is daddy not answering or just stepping into the tub
a few pictures hang memories
the walls stand upright
baby opens the door
daddy shuts it
mamma sits in the closet and cries
a book topples over
daddy has only one shoe on
a fly crawls up the window pane
it gets dark
the floor lamp is kicked and
radiates matter-of-fact light
the doorbell rings the ave maria by bach-gounod
baby's finally asleep
daddy opens the door

(1966)

description of nature

clouds frown
flowers grow pale
fields turn a cold shoulder
paths crawl into a corner
stones stare blindly
mountains sink into silence
valleys shudder
a gust of wind escapes from the air
rivers step over their banks
shrubs tear their leaves
trees throw up their branches

earth totters into the night

(1979)

the shortest route
from constanz to constantinople

constanz
constany
constanx
constanw
constanv
constanu
constant
constanti
constantin
constantino
constantinop
constantinopl
constantinople

(1979)

group dynamics

anton drops his pants like an antelope
bertha drops her pants like a bobolink
caesar drops his pants like a camembert
dora drops her pants like a dahlia
emil drops his pants like an expert
frederic drops his pants like free trade
gustav drops his pants like a gallowsbird
henry drops his pants like a havenothing
ida drops her pants like an illusion
julius drops his pants like a kilowatt
ludwig drops his pants like a lab assistant
martha drops her pants on the north pole—
otto drops his pants like an obelisk
paula drops her pants like a quotation mark
richard drops his pants like a rabbi
sam drops his pants on schedule
theodor drops his pants like a tobacco company
ulrich drops his pants like an ultimatum
victor drops his pants like a vagabond
willie drops his pants like a whooping cough
xanthippe drops her pants like yesterday
zachary drops his pants like a zucchini
says "that's that"
and puts his pants back on
and xanthippe puts her pants back on like zachary
and willie puts his pants back on like zanthippe
and victor puts his pants back on like willie
and ulrich puts his pants back on like victor
and theodor puts his pants back on like ulrich
and sam puts his pants back on like theodor
and richard puts his pants back on like sam
and paula puts her pants back on like richard

and otto puts his pants back on like paula
and martha puts her pants back on like otto
and ludwig puts his pants back on like martha
and julius puts his pants back on like ludwig
and ida puts her pants back on like julius
and henry puts his pants back on like ida
and gustav puts his pants back on like henry
and frederic puts his pants back on like gustav
and emil puts his pants back on like frederic
and dora puts her pants back on like emil
and caesar puts his pants back on like dora
and bertha puts her pants back on like caesar
but anton stays bareassed

(1982)

nature morte

the table stands
the chair sits
the bed lies
the clock runs
the glass cracks
the temperature drops

(1977/84)

litany for good friday

o god, are we more than robots?
o god, are we just robots?
o god, why just robots?
o god, and so primitive?
o god, why so primitive?
o god, no chance?
o god, just like that?
o god, so limited?
o god, why so limited?
o god, why so primitive and limited?
o god, why such limited robots?
o god, so unable to learn?
o god, so unteachable?
o god, why such primitive robots if we must be robots?
o god, why such limited, unteachable robots?
o god, robots, robots!
o god, robots only!
simple robots.
shoddy.
clods.
o god!

(1985)

lovesong for lily

in limelight little lily
her lithe limbs lying on lilywhite linen
with lifted lids and licking limber lips
limns left to right in lilting lines
the limpid litany of love, literally:
love love love...

(1986)

***susanna's
rhyming compulsion***

susanna in a chair
washes her hair.
susanna in bichlorid
washes her forehead.
susanna asks why
should i wash my eye?
susanna in tears
washes her ears.
susanna in hose
washes her nose.
susanna up the creek
washes her cheek.
susanna down south
washes her mouth.
susanna forsooth
brushes her tooth.
susanna feeling raw
washes her jaw.
susanna when stung
washes her tongue.
susanna from a tin
washes her chin.
with a high note
she rinses her throat.
if given a peck
she washes her neck.
then asks her friend jack
to scrub her back.
is susanna happiest
when she washes her breast?
in any case her heart's

in washing her warts.
susanna in jelly
washes her belly.
susanna with chips
washes her hips.
susanna with grass
wipes her ass.
susanna gets blunt
and washes her cunt.
susanna when warm
washes her arm.
susanna cries
washing her thighs.
overcome by ennui
she washes her knee.
she composes her epitaph
when washing her calf.
susanna takes off her boot
to wash her foot.
susanna on the go
washes her toe.

(1989)

VI. ALBERTUS MAGNUS:
A RELIQUARY HISTORY AS BOOK OF HOURS

As Albert, At An Advanced Age, lectured one day in the monastery of the predicants to A large Audience, he suddenly lost his memory. All the audience were taken Aback. Albert, however, After having been silent for a while, offered — released from the narrow I of memories — the following explanation: "All mye life I strove towarde the now, And..."

Albert's corpse was (According to his wishes) placed prone, As if prostrate in prayer, into a wooden casket in front of the steps of the high Altar of the holy cross church in cologne. The wooden casket was placed into A stone coffin. the stone coffin was lowered into A ditch. earth was thrown on it. A stone plaque was pressed on top so that it stuck up from the ground by the breadth of A hand. A fence was erected Around it.
"here lieth Albert,
phoenix Among the learned,
incomparable,
prince of philosophers,
vessel whence floweth doctrine of sacred wordes."
without Address,
without Adenoids,
without Advertisement,
without Alarm clock,
without Ammunition,
without Amontillado,
without Anchor chain,
without Answers,
without Ashtray,
without Atlas,
without Atom bomb,
without Automobile.

Brother salvus cassetta from palermo had the grave opened with iron implements on 11 january 1483. albert's Body was covered with earth Because the lid of the wooden Box had rotted away in the intervening 203 years. after the earth had Been removed the intact Body was taken out and Brought to light.
it had
1 Bishop's crosier in its hand,
1 copper ring on its finger,
sandals on its feet,
1 Bishop's miter on its head,
the eyes that, in alemanic swabia, had seen the stone where more than five hundred snakes had gathered before Being cut to pieces by the swords of soldiers to clear a path for the lord of the land and where at the bottom there had lain a huge snake, now also cut to pieces, under whose head there had Been a Black pyramid-shape stone with a picture of this very snake, which the wife of the lord of that land had given albert as a present together with the head of the snake, were still in their sockets,
on the chin there remained some flesh with part of the Beard,
1 ear, with which he had heard the song of a swan lamenting his dead mate, had shriveled,
the shoulders showed no sign of decay,
1 upper arm was practically intact,
the thighs that still had desiccated flesh clinging to them were likewise noticed,
around the neck which still contained the trachea there hung
1 particle from the cross of the lord
1 coin pierced by one of the nails of the lord
1 agnus dei of wax wrapped in silk,
no Bacon,
no Bank Book,
no Bar stool,
no Barbecued chicken

no Bath towel,
no Battery,
no Bedding,
no Beer can,
no Bicarbonate of soda,
no Bicycle,
no Broom,
no Bucket.

on raising the corpse salvus cassetta took
albert's upper right arm
to Bring to the pope. after the death of pope sixtus IV the upper arm was Brought to Bologna and placed next to the head of dominicus, founder of the dominican order.
albert's corpse minus the upper right arm was exhibited in a glass shrine.

Camping ground?
Catsup?
Chambre séparée?
6 Chemicals?
1 Chronometer?
1 Computer?
1 Couch?
1 bone, half a finger wide, from albert's left arm
bishop albert IV was permitted, on 18 january 1619, after a battle of two years, to take from the Cologne shrine for the Cathedral of regensburg. as an ardent admirer of his name patron he had actually "with burning desyre" hoped for "the most sacred heade" because "he had learned that unto one most venerable nuntius had been given an entyre arm."

Detestable swedes, in 1633, conquered and Despoiled regensburg, and the bone from albert's arm Disappeared from the cathedral. as replacement regensburg received from the Dean of the predicant brothers in cologne the Donation of
1 rib of albert's
which on 13 December 1654 was solemnly moved from the Dominican convent, where it had been Displayed after transfer, to the cathedral.

not 1 Death mask,
not 1 Derby,
not 7 Dia projectors,
not 1 Dime,
not 1 Donut,
not 1 Doornail.

Effluvia of progressive putrefaction had been observed. on 29 september 1671, therefore, the glass shrine had to be opened and Emptied.

the smaller relics were added to a silver Effigy of albert and Encased in a silver Ewer,

the larger bones, Enshrined in a wooden casket 4 foot long and 2 foot high and Edged in silver.

these new reliquaries were kept in the sacristy so that on holidays they could be Easily Exhibited on the high altar.

1 Earphone
1 Eau de cologne
1 Echocardiogram
3 Eggs
1 Electric toy train
4 Emetics
1 Eraser

were not Entered into the shrine.

For the chapel of the suffragan bishop of regensburg there was removed from the reopened casket on 2 july 1693
1 shoulderblade of albert's.
For the papal nuntius, archbishop of thebes, who had presided over the opening,
1 unlabeled bone, Fractured, and
the lower portion of the crosier.
in compensation thereof
neither 1 Facade
nor 1 Fahrenheit
neither 1 Fan
nor 1 Farthing
neither 1 Feather
nor 1 Ferriswheel
neither 1 Fever thermometer
nor 1 Fire extinguisher
neither 1 Fishing rod
nor 1 Flashlight
neither 1 Football
nor 1 Fork
were added to the casket before it was resealed.

Gouged open once again was the casket toward 4 o'clock in the afternoon of 30 september 1767 in order to sever from albert's corpse first
2 sections of the skull
of which one — an almost rectangular piece of cranium of 10 x 18 cm — was destined to Go to the vicar of lauingen who had begged for relics for his church "so that the fervor and devotion to saint albert should inextinguishable rendered be," the other to be Given to anton ignaz, imperial count of fugger and provost of ellwangen.
on this occasion there was also severed from the corpse
1 bone
for the dominican church in sittart as well as
1 part of a rib
for the convent church of st. Gertrude in cologne.
remained unmentioned
1 Garage
1 Garden hose
1 Gas mask
1 Gearshift
1 Gimlet
3 Gloves
1 Golf ball
1 Guarantee Slip
1 Guest register
1 Gyroscope.

Had the rest of the cranium been removed from the casket
on 25 february 1775, it was Hastily followed Hardly 2 years later,
on 22 january 1777, by
3 remains of ribs. Of
1 Hair pin
2 Hand grenades
5 Hearing trumpets
1 Helicopter
1 Hobbyhorse
1 Hurdy-gurdy
no mention was made in either case.

In the year 1804, when the destroyed church of the holy cross was demolished, the black wooden casket with the remaining bones of albert — though without Its silver edges — could be saved and transported to st. andrew's where It was at first placed In the choir on the gospel side, later In the northern transept.
the church of the holy cross had already been desecrated In 1802 during the napoleonic occupation.
10 Interstate highways could have found room Inside It as well as Insect powder and
1 Insulating tape of considerable length.

(Job lot
Just

Kindred to a chapel in form, with pediments on the narrow sides and center, the lateral surfaces divided by buttresses into 8 niches each, carved in oak and partly gilded, such is the precious gothic reliquary where the contents of albert's worm-eaten box were relocated on 14 november 1859.

on raising the remains there were found in the old wooden casket:

the upper jaw with petrosal bone and 4 teeth,

the lower jaw with 11 teeth — the very same that once when albert, 5 centuries ago, while slurping an oyster tasted the smell of the sea, bit on 10 pearls,

the right petrosal bone,

the major part of the skull,

the left collar bone,

37 ribs or parts of ribs,

the 1st bone of the sternum

21 vertebrae,

the sacrum,

2 lateral parts of the pelvis (ilium, ischium and pubis),

the left shoulderblade,

the upper and lower outer part of an upper arm,

the right ulna,

2 fragments of a fibula,

1 metacarpal,

1 1st thumb bone,

2 femurs,

2 shinbones,

1 fragment of a fibula,

thyroid cartilage,

2 fragments of the cranium

1 silk pillow with a peculiar weave

the document of 2 june 1693 pertaining to removal of the left shoulderblade,

4 fragments of a wooden crozier with iron tip,

plus chasuble,

stole and maniple.
1 Kalendar,
1 Komb,
2 Kandles,
1 Klavier,
2 Koathangers,
1 Koffer,
Kologne,
1 Korkscrew,
1 Kravat were not found among them.
dressed in albert's chasuble bishop baudri consecrated a new altar into which the precious shrine was ceremoniously incorporated. with the exception of the 1st thumb bone, which was earmarked for the altar of st.albert, all the pieces reposing in their new dwelling had been fastened to red silk.

Living matter dies quickly; dead matter, Like
1 Ladder,
1 Ladle
1 Lamp,
1 Latch,
1 Lens,
1 Lever,
2 Lightbulbs,
1 Linchpin
1 Lipstick,
1 Lock
1 Loud-speaker
often somewhat more slowly.
in 1891 there was removed from albert's new shrine
the index finger that once on a beach had touched a jellyfish which had spread Like eggwhite and collapsed, but on being returned to the water had regained its hemispherical form and moved on by means of alternating expansion and contraction.
this index finger was transferred to bonn, which at present is the seat of the german federal government.

Mouthing the words "thus i became." albert — called Magnus, the great — left his lectern. under one eye he had a birth Mark, in his Middle, his navel.

10 Machine guns,
1 Mask,
1 Microphone.

1 Metacarpal,
1 Major fragment of a rib,
2 fragments of fibula, 16 cm and 12 cm, and
some very small unidentifiable fragments of bones
were removed from albert's remains as late as 27 june 1932 on the occasion of an inspection of the relics, before they, together with
bone dust
gathered in a small bag, were couched in two Metal containers with gold lids 22 cm high, 18.5 cm deep, 55 cm long and thus reintegrated into the large gothic shrine.
on 15 november 1954 the two Metal casettes containing the essential remains were placed in a lead coffin lined with oak. this coffin presently reposes in a roman stone sarcophagus in the crypt excavated after world war II under the sanctuary of st. andrew's.

the time of removal of
1 tooth
is uncertain.

on the occasion of the transfer Measurements were taken of the decayed bones which — taking into account albert's advanced age and the decomposition of the corpse — yielded the following size for albert's body:

|''''|''''|''''|''''|''''|''''|''''|''''|''''|''''|''''|''''|''''|''''|''''|''''|''''|''''|''''|''''|''''|''''|''''|''''|

No)

according to a. m.: "that which existeth from the beginning hath influence on all that followeth."
of the methods of divination by the four elements he practiced geomancy. To effect the puncturing of the earth two tables are Needed, the first of which contains all questions permissible in daylight. the answers repose in the
Night

0

P

Q

R

S

T

V

W

X

Y

Zoom:

NOTE

Gerhard Rühm was born in Vienna in 1930. He began by studying composition and Oriental music, performing "noise-music" and "one-tone-compositions," but came to devote most of his energy to literature. As early as the 1950s, he got interested in visual poetry and established contact between his "Wiener Gruppe" and concrete poets elsewhere. Unlike other members of the Vienna Group he has always been intent on working out the theoretical foundations of his experiments and can be called one of the initiators of the "linguistic turn" in the avantgarde. His aim has been nothing less than a renewal of literature through the materiality of language which, stripped of its communication-based conventions, is to become an aesthetic medium on a par with music and visual art.

Rühm is also known for his editions of Baroque and Expressionist poets, and of Konrad Bayer's work. His prizes include the "Grosse Österreichische Staatspreis" (1991) and the "Hörspielpreis der Kriegsblinden" (1983). From 1972-95 he was professor at the Hamburg Academy of Fine Arts. He now lives in Cologne.

If the world is language for Rühm, the dictionary is its body, and the alphabet its backbone. His novel, *Textall,* for instance, contains the entire vocabulary of a German-Japanese dictionary. The "theatrical events" of *Reisefieber* [*Cabin Fever*] chart travel to 5 foreign cities by choosing their vocabulary exclusively from the letter "a" in a dictionary of the language in question. All the words in "Moscow" are German equivalents of Russian words starting with "a" — and are used in the order they appear in *Langenscheidt's Russian-German Pocket Dictionary.*

His effort to find forms that accomodate precise cognition along with experience have led him to study Christian mystics and combinatorial patterns in mathematics. Both have fed into "Albertus Magnus" (who is the patron saint of Cologne and its university). Here the alphabet is pitted against the cult of relics in the Catholic church, which turned Albertus Magnus's body into an almost inexhaustible inventory of bones.

In his postface to this work, Rühm states:

"my 'history' begins with the moment when albert loses his memory, i.e. his biography. the following chronicle of decay and dispersion of his bodily remains (in twelve stations, the number that structures the text) merely documents the universal law of entropy in action. still, even the few albertian bones and bits of dust are tiny particles of our self-destructive civilization. relics, the manifest and palpable mementos of a man who once could see, hear, feel, smell and taste — this is what the inserted quotations from albertus are meant to make present...."

"the alphabet in 'albertus' has only 24 letters — in albertus' lifetime, j and i, u and v were used interchangeably for the same sound. so the letters can be correlated with the 24 hours of one day-and-night cycle. considering his initials, there is an attractive symbolic relation between the name 'Albertus Magnus' and daytime ('a' to 'm' is exactly half this alphabet) — again in the sense of a 'book of hours.' the second, nighttime half of the alphabet closes the circle..."

Rühm has remained a radical experimenter, a restless explorer of traditions and genres, atomizing their elements in order to recompose them with conceptual precision and a multiplicity of compositional techniques. His recent work includes *Pencil Music*, a CD from Hundertmark-Gallery that transforms drawing into an acoustic event.

Rosmarie Waldrop's most recent books of poetry are *Blindsight* (New Directions) and *Love, Like Pronouns* (Omnidawn). Her memoir, *Lavish Absence: Recalling and Rereading Edmond Jabès* was published by Wesleyan University Press. She has translated books by Edmond Jabès, Jacques Roubaud, Emmanuel Hocquard from the French and, from the German, Friederike Mayröcker, Elke Erb, Oskar Pastior.